Self-Worth Essentials

A Workbook to Understand Yourself,
Accept Yourself, Like Yourself, Respect Yourself,
Be Confident, Enjoy Yourself, and Love Yourself

Ж

Liisa Kyle, Ph.D.

Shimmer Press

Ж

Copyright © Liisa Kyle, Ph.D., 2016

Ж

All rights reserved. No part of this product may be reproduced, scanned, or distributed in any printed or electronic form without permission.

Thank you for respecting the professional work and intellectual property of this author. If you know someone who would benefit from this book, be kind: either recommend it to them or buy them their own copy.

ISBN: 978-1535123839

Ж

This book is licensed solely for your personal enjoyment and private self-reflection. This material is not intended as psychological counseling or as a professional coaching relationship with Liisa Kyle, Ph.D. If you require clinical help, please contact a qualified professional immediately.

Contents

Chapter 1 - Yes, You Are Worth It..1

Chapter 2 - Seven Essential Phases of Self-Worth.................................3

Chapter 3 - Phase One: Understand Yourself...5

Chapter 4 - Phase Two: Accept Yourself...15

Chapter 5 - Phase Three: Like Yourself..27

Chapter 6 - Phase Four: Respect Yourself..33

Chapter 7 - Phase Five: Be Confident in Yourself...............................47

Chapter 8 - Phase Six: Enjoy Yourself..61

Chapter 9 - Phase Seven: Love Yourself..71

About the Author...81

Chapter 1

Yes, You Are Worth It

Self-esteem is how you see yourself.

Self-worth is how you value yourself.

As a Ph.D. in Psychology and a life coach, I've spent the last twenty years working with smart, accomplished people. It never fails to surprise me how many of these successful people harbor doubts about their self-worth.

Some question or downplay their talents. Others crave external validation — they seek any scrap of praise or approval from others. Some are "People Pleasers" doing too much for other people, to their own detriment. Others don't really like themselves, deep down. They find fault with themselves easily. They are overly harsh with themselves. They have a sense that they could be better or different than they perceive themselves to be. It's more than feeling like an imposter: Deep down, they feel that they're not really worthy of love or success or both.

They are wrong.

Everyone is worthy of love. Everyone is worthy of success.

Over the past twenty years, I've devised practical techniques to improve people's perceptions of themselves (i.e. their self-esteem) as well as their self-worth (the extent to which they value themselves.) I've designed this workbook to guide you through the seven essential phases of improving your self-worth.

This book is for you if you would like to:

- understand yourself better
- accept those things you like least about yourself
- like yourself more
- treat yourself better
- improve your self-confidence
- find new ways to enjoy being you, and
- learn to love yourself

Yes, you're worth it. Let's get started.

Ж

How to Get the Most Out of This Workbook

There are thousands of ways to improve your self-worth. I've designed this book to be an efficient sampling of the techniques I've found to be the most effective. I'm presenting these "essentials" in a workbook format so you can actually work through the activities right on these pages.

There are many **"Key Questions"** for you to contemplate and answer as a way of gaining new insights about yourself.

There are also some **"Deep Dive Activities"** designed to plumb a little deeper. Ideally, you will set aside uninterrupted time to give these questions your full, focused attention.

As well, there are some **"Fieldwork Activities"** i.e. things for you to do. These are practical assignments for you to implement in your life.

I encourage you to **work your way through all the activities in this workbook** in the order in which they appear. Go through the process at whatever pace is comfortable for you. For maximum effectiveness, actually **write out your answers** in the spaces provided. By putting pen to paper, you will elicit more and better insights. The more you write, the more successful you will be in improving your self-worth.

Chapter 2

Seven Essential Phases of Self-Worth

Take a moment to think of someone you don't particularly like. This might be someone in your life or a public figure you disdain. If you don't like them, odds are, you don't respect them. If you don't respect them, you likely don't value them very highly.

In the same way, it's impossible to value or love yourself if, deep down, you don't really like yourself. Imagine the development of self-worth as a broad path from self-knowledge through self-acceptance to self-respect and eventually to self-love.

Actually, there are a few more steps involved. In my work over the past twenty years, I've found there are

Seven Essential Phases of Self-Worth:

Phase One is to **Understand Yourself**. Until you have an accurate picture of yourself, you have little basis to value yourself.

Phase Two is to **Accept Yourself**. When you are okay with who you really are, you can begin to truly appreciate yourself. This means acknowledging your strengths as well as your failings. All humans have flaws. If you want to improve your self-worth, you must accept yours.

As you begin to accept yourself, Phase Three is to **Like Yourself**. You know you're at this phase when you acknowledge and express your favorite aspects of yourself.

The more you like yourself, the more you will merit self-respect. Phase Four is to **Respect Yourself**. You will treat yourself well — and you will expect others to do the same.

As you treat yourself better, with respect and appreciation, you will learn to **Be Confident in Yourself**, which is Phase Five. You will feel capable and complete. You will leave behind fears, doubts, and the need for external validation.

Phase Six is to **Enjoy Yourself**. To delight in being you. To have fun. To celebrate what's important to you.

Phase Seven is the culmination of all the previous phases: it is to **Love Yourself**. This means to care about yourself. To be your own best friend. To know and believe your true worth.

The rest of this book contains practical activities to guide you through each of the seven essential phases of self-worth.

Ж

Chapter 3

Phase One: Understand Yourself

The first essential step in bolstering your self-esteem and self-worth is to examine yourself. You can't truly appreciate yourself until you understand who you really are.

This chapter offers plentiful opportunities to understand yourself better. Note that there may seem to be some overlap between some of the sections: This is by design so that you can examine different aspects of your life in different ways.

Self-Perspective

Let's begin by seeing how you view yourself.

Please clear some uninterrupted time to answer the following questions. The more thought you give, the more you'll get out of this process. For maximum effectiveness, write out your answers. If you do, you will generate more ideas and better quality insights.

KEY QUESTIONS:

1. How do you describe yourself?

2. What do you like best about yourself?

3. What strengths do you use most often?

4. What do you like least about yourself?

5. List your skills and talents.

6. To what extent are you open to new experiences?

7. Would you describe yourself as someone who is strong, driven, and dominant . . . or would you describe yourself differently? How so?

8. To what extent are you outgoing, social, or extraverted?

9. To what extent are you shy or introverted? In which circumstances are you more so? Less so?

10. How do you get in your own way?

11. How do you handle conflict in your personal relationships?

12. How do you handle conflict in your professional relationships?

Self-Worth Essentials

DEEP DIVE ACTIVITY: YOUR ESSENTIAL SELF

Clear five minutes for private, uninterrupted reflection.

Ask yourself: Who are you, deep down? How would you describe your essential self? *Hint: This might be different from how you behave in your present circumstances.* Jot down whatever words or phrases pop into your head to describe your "real" self.

FIELDWORK ACTIVITY:

This week, look for opportunities to show off your essential self.

Find ways to be who you really are, deep down. For example: If your core self is "playful", then make a point of having some extra fun. Find humor in your day. Treat yourself to some guilt-free play. If, at heart, you are "loving", find ways to express extra affection to those you care about. Commit random acts of kindness. Show yourself some love.

Others' Perspective

It's illuminating to examine how you see yourself. It can be even more enlightening to learn how others see you.

> **KEY QUESTIONS:**
>
> 1. How do others describe you? What words or phrases do they tend to use?
>
>
>
> 2. What compliments do you hear most often about yourself?
>
>
>
> 3. What criticisms do you hear most often about yourself?

FIELDWORK ACTIVITY: ASK FOR FEEDBACK

1. Choose a few trusted people for their feedback. Ideally, you'd like information from people who know you in different circumstances. For example, you might ask someone who knows you personally, someone who knows you professionally, someone who knows you socially, and someone who is intimately familiar with you. **Be prudent** in your choices: Choose people you trust and respect. Avoid asking anyone who makes you feel uncomfortable in any way.

    I choose the following trusted people:

2. Contact each person you've selected and communicate your version of the following:

    I'm seeking some personal feedback. I'd appreciate it if you would answer the following questions about me:
    What words would you use to describe me?
    What do you like best about me?
    What suggestions for improvement do you have for me?
    Anything you can send my way by next Friday would be much appreciated. Thank you.

    Use this space to write your preferred version of the example:

3. When you receive responses, make a point of thanking the sender. Any feedback you receive — positive, negative or neutral — is a gift because it's an opportunity to learn more about yourself.

4. Process the responses you receive by answering the following questions:

   - What confirms how you see yourself?

   - What differs from how you view yourself?

   - Any surprises?

   - Anything requiring follow-up? *For example, if you don't understand a comment, ask for clarification and/or examples. If someone reveals something requiring action, a conversation, an apology, or amends, make a point of doing so within a week. Again, thank the person for the opportunity to improve your relationship — and yourself.*

Self-Worth Essentials

The most powerful words are the ones we use to describe ourselves. We might not even be aware of what those words are — or where they came from.

The following activity is a powerful one adapted from *Vein of Gold* by Julia Cameron. In it you will consider the words that other people have labeled you in the past. These words can shape how we think about ourselves. For example, maybe when you were a kid, someone called you "scattered" or "bossy." Maybe it hurt. Perhaps you laughed. Either way, you may have inadvertently internalized the label.

This activity is meant to check what self-labels you have inside . . . and then to process them accordingly. If something stings, there is an opportunity to examine it. Question the validity of any hurtful or negative label. It might not be true. It might not be accurate. It was just that person's opinion at that time — and probably said more about their issues and personality than it did about you.

The next step is to convert any negative label into a more helpful, more accurate one. For example "scattered" could be re-written as "interested in many things." "Bossy" could be re-written as "strong."

When I did this exercise, it triggered a clear memory of the occasion when an elementary school chum expressed her exasperation that I "start all these different projects and never finish any of them!" She called me a "flake." It hurt. This unexpected recollection revealed a negative label that, to my surprise, I'd been carrying deep inside for decades.

As soon as I identified it, I could question its validity. The truth is that sure I was involved in a lot of activities as a kid. Yes, I started many different projects. However I finished many of them. (And what did my projects have to do with her? Why was she so bothered by them?) The cosmic Truth is that no one *has* to finish *everything* they start. In fact, the physical reality is that it's absolutely impossible to do so.

Okay, my school chum thought I was a flake (and probably still does), but that label isn't accurate. I'm not a flake. I'm quite conscientious and responsible. However, I do have a lot going on. I do start a lot of projects. Some don't get finished. A more accurate label would be that I'm "interested in many things." It's true! I am interested in many things! I'll shout it proudly!

It was helpful to identify the negative label I'd unwittingly internalized. It was satisfying indeed to exorcise it and to transform it into a more helpful, pleasant description. I invite you to do the same using the process on page 13.

PHASE ONE: UNDERSTAND YOURSELF

DEEP DIVE ACTIVITY: REWRITE LABELS

Write down some negative labels you recall from childhood (*e.g., bossy*)	Is this true? Is this accurate? What evidence is there to the contrary?	Convert these negative words into more helpful, accurate interpretations (*e.g., strong*)

FIELDWORK ACTIVITY:

Post your more helpful, accurate labels somewhere where you will see them often. *E.g., on a Post-It in your planner or wallet; in your phone, tablet, or computer.*

Chapter 4

Phase Two: Accept Yourself

It's easy enough to accept those things we like about ourselves — and we'll spend Chapter 5 focusing on them. The real challenge of self-acceptance is coming to terms with those aspects of ourselves that we dislike. In this chapter we'll explore essential ways to accept those aspects of yourself that you like the least.

It's not pleasant to consider the things we don't like about ourselves, but it's necessary that we do so. We can't truly accept ourselves unless we come to terms with who we are.

Ж

Key Question: What Don't I Like About Myself?

What do you like least about yourself? What is there about you that you wish was different? What don't you like about yourself?

Consider:

- aspects of your personality

- things you find yourself doing when you know better

- things that are contrary to your "preferred self"

- how you treat certain people

SELF-WORTH ESSENTIALS

- how you do certain tasks

- things you've done or said in the past

- ruts you've fallen into

- unhealthy or unhelpful beliefs or thought patterns

- unhealthy or unhelpful habits or patterns of behavior

- things about yourself about which you are embarrassed, ashamed, sad, or guilty

---

KEY QUESTION:

Make a list: What do you like least about yourself? What is there about you that you wish was different? What don't you like about yourself?

When you actually make your list, congratulate yourself. You've made a huge step towards self-acceptance. Let's more forward swiftly to process this information. First, let's conduct a reality check.

Key Question: Is This True?

Sometimes when we make lists like this, we tend to exaggerate or over generalize. For example, if you wrote "I've wasted my education" on your list, that's probably an exaggeration. Surely you're using *some* of your education. You are using your ability to read this page, for example. Maybe a more accurate statement is something like "I believe I should be making more money and receiving more recognition for my efforts, given my knowledge and expertise."

KEY QUESTION: IS THIS TRUE?

Review the list you made on the previous page. As you read each item, ask: Is this really true?

Cross off anything that is not true.

Re-word anything that is over generalized, exaggerated, or otherwise inaccurate. Be as specific as possible. Here's space to do so:

Why do this? The more specific you are, the more accurately you can process the information. For example, let's say you wrote "I hate my face" in answer to question #1 and that you revised this in answer to question #2 to something more specific like "I don't like the ruddy patches on my cheeks or the shape of my ears." First, you've reduced the scope of your dislike: You don't hate your entire face — just the color of your cheeks and the shape of your ears. Second, you've zeroed in on something that's changeable. There are medications and cosmetics designed to reduce skin redness. If you chose to, you *could* change the shape of your ears via surgery.

This brings us to the next key question.

Ж

Key Question: Is This Changeable?

When you consider your least favorite aspects of yourself, some are changeable and some are not.

Things you've said or done in the past are not changeable. Much as we would like to, we cannot alter what's happened. We can learn from the experience. We can apologize. We can make amends. But we can't undo deeds or un-say words.

For the most part, aspects of your personality are impervious to change. Research has shown that the extent to which you are dominant, agreeable, or conscientious is pretty much set for life. Same for whether you are extraverted or introverted; outgoing or private; intense or easy-going.

This is where acceptance comes in. If something is unchangeable, the only option is to accept it . . . otherwise you'll make yourself miserable.

KEY QUESTION: IS THIS CHANGEABLE?

Review your revised list on page 17.

For each item, ask: Is this changeable?

Put a checkmark beside anything you can change.

Put an "X" beside anything you can't change.

Key Question: How Else Could I Look at This?

If something is changeable, then you have possible remedies available. If you feel strongly enough about it, you will take action to change this thing you don't like about yourself. (We'll get to that in the next section.)

For now, let's focus on those things you cannot change. If something is unchangeable — or if you choose to not change it — then how can you come to accept it about yourself?

One solution is to learn to think differently about it. Consider this admittedly trite example: "I hate my jiggly thighs" is much less helpful or healthy than "I'm in better shape than many people my age. It's unrealistic to expect to have a body like Jennifer Lawrence. She's 5'9" and 26 years old, for heaven's sake. Okay, sure I don't look like a Hollywood star but I also don't want to put up with their diet restrictions or onerous fitness regimes. Plus I don't have teams of people paid to make me look good (such as stylists, dieticians, personal trainers, marketers, Photoshoppers, and surgeons) so it's unreasonable to expect my legs to look as if I did. Heck I'm happy to just HAVE legs — my life would be very different without them. I'm mobile. I'm physically active. My thighs are plenty 'good enough'. I accept them as they are."

Consider each unchangeable thing from different perspectives. For example, if you regret something in the past, consider that you did the best you could at the time, given the skills, knowledge, and resources you had available at that time.

Did some good come out of it? Was there a silver lining? A lesson learned?

Are there one or more upsides to it? There might be something about this aspect of yourself that's actually positive. For example, maybe you don't really like that you're a grump — but you realize that because of your grumpiness, people are less likely to take advantage of you.

Another approach is to consider things from the perspectives of others — none of whom, I promise you, are viewing you as harshly as you do yourself. For example, are there people who love you, regardless of your grumpiness? Heck, they might even love you *because* of your grumpiness.

Consider someone you know who also has this feature that you don't like about yourself. Are there people who love them anyway? Their parents, their spouse, their children, their friends? Of course there are. Same goes for you. No matter what you see as being your flaws, someone loves you. And some may even find this quality endearing. "Oh Krista is such a prickly pear! It's funny how she sees things — and she doesn't take any guff from anyone. I know she has my back."

Self-Worth Essentials

Those aspects of yourself you don't particularly like may well be the things that others love the most about you. Or maybe this horrible fault you think you have is completely invisible to anyone else. Ha! It might just be a self-misperception.

DEEP DIVE ACTIVITY: EXAMINING THE UNCHANGEABLE

Pick one unchangeable item from your list on page 17. With this in mind, answer the following questions:

1. What is the impact on you to not accept this unchangeable item? How does it affect you?

2. Is there another way to look at this item? What might be a more helpful perspective?

3. Consider what might be the upsides of this item. *(For example, if "I'm getting older" is on your list, some upsides might be "I'm wiser than I've ever been; I've got a more informed perspective; I've got rich experiences from which to draw; I've collected more valued relationships; I'm making better decisions; etc.")*

4. How might someone close to you view this item? *(For example, imagine you made a mistake you are having a hard time getting over. Someone else might see your "mistake" as a learning opportunity — or you being human — or you doing the best you could with the skills and information you had available at that time.)*

5. Consider someone you know who also has this feature. List some people who love them anyway.

6. Do you owe anyone (or yourself) an apology for this item? If so, ask for forgiveness. Write out an apology. If you can deliver the apology, all the better. But it doesn't matter if that's not possible. Apologize anyway.

7. Are there amends that can be made for this item? If so, make them.

8. What would be the benefits to you if you accepted this thing about yourself?

9. Choose to accept this thing you cannot change.

DEEP DIVE ACTIVITY: EXAMINING THE UNCHANGEABLE

Make enough photocopies of pages 22 and 23 so that you can repeat the process with each unchangeable item on your list on page 17. I recommend you break this into separate sessions on different days. In each session, pick a different unchangeable item.

Today's focus is: _____

1. What is the impact on you to not accept this unchangeable item? How does it affect you?

2. Is there another way to look at this item? What might be a more helpful perspective?

3. Consider what might be the upsides of this item.

4. How might someone close to you view this item?

5. Consider someone you know who also has this feature. List some people who love them anyway.

6. Do you owe anyone (or yourself) an apology for this item? If so, ask for forgiveness. Write out an apology. If you can deliver the apology, all the better. But it doesn't matter if that's not possible. Apologize anyway.

7. Are there amends that can be made for this item? If so, make them.

8. What would be the benefits to you if you accepted this thing about yourself?

9. Choose to accept this thing you cannot change.

Once you have worked through the unchangeable items on your list, you can turn to those that are changeable. These might include a rut you've found yourself in, unhealthy habits, or unhelpful patterns of behavior. The challenge here is that to change these items, you must really want to change them.

Ж

Key Question: Do I *Really* Want to Change This Thing?

Let's say you've identified an unhealthy habit you have. Do you really want to curtail or eliminate it? To make a change you need a vision of what you want, clear first steps to take, and enough motivation to overcome the inevitable resistance that will arise, once you embark on the change.

If you want to change something — really want to change it — then do so. (If it's helpful, I've written a workbook entitled *You Can Change Your Life* to guide you through that process.) But be candid with yourself: Are you ready to do what it takes to make this change or not?

Let's say you're not thrilled with the ten pounds that have crept onto your torso in the past few years. Are you willing to exercise and to restrict your food consumption to whittle away the excess? If so, stop grumbling about your waistline and do something about it. Action will feel much better than thinking ill of yourself. But if you can't get up the gumption to get to the gym, then it mustn't be that important to you. Instead, accept your waistline as it is.

Sure, you'd rather your ears were a different shape. But are you really so bothered by them that you're willing to undergo surgery? If so, do so. If not, then accept your ears' appearance, once and for all.

Accept the things you've decided not to change.

On the following page is a process to work through the changeable items on the list you made on page 17. Make enough photocopies of page 25 so that you can work through each item separately.

Work through your list at a pace that is comfortable for you. Some items will require more thought and reflection than others. Do what makes sense for each item.

Ж

DEEP DIVE ACTIVITY: EXAMINING THE CHANGEABLE

Pick one changeable item from your list on page 17.

Today's focus is: _____

1. How badly do you want to change this item on a scale of one to ten, where "1" means "not at all" and "10" means "very much so"?

2. What are you willing to do to change it?

3. What are you not willing to do to change it?

4. Given your answers to the first three questions, what makes sense? Will you change this thing or will you accept it?

    If you choose to accept it, take a moment and truly do so.

    If you choose to change it: Devise and implement a plan to do so. What needs to happen? *(There's more space to write on the next page.)*

Chapter 5

Phase Three: Like Yourself

In the previous chapter, we focused on essential ways to come to terms with those parts of yourself you like least. This chapter is much more fun: It's an opportunity to acknowledge and express your favorite aspects of yourself.

Ж

Key Question: What Do I Like Best About Myself?

Give yourself this gift: spend time considering and appreciating your favorite features. What do you like most about yourself? This might include:

- aspects of your personality

- things about yourself that make you happy

- things about you that are aligned with your "preferred self"

- your skills and talents

- how you treat certain people

- how you do certain tasks

- healthy or helpful beliefs or thought patterns

- healthy or helpful habits or patterns of behavior

KEY QUESTION:

What are your favorite aspects of yourself? Make a list.

Key Question: Am I Expressing My Favorite Features?

Once you remind yourself of your favorite features, the next question is this: to what extent are you experiencing these parts of yourself in your current life?

For example, let's say that you like your intelligence. To what extent are you using your brain these days? It might be that you have ample opportunities to put your thinking skills to good, productive use . . . or it might be that you need more intellectual stimulation.

If you need to use your mind more, the next question would be how can you do so, given your current life situation and personal preferences? Are there opportunities at work or in your personal life? Some people might be drawn to crossword puzzles or computer word games. Others might seek out local classes or a chess club. Can you take a class or teach one? What volunteer activities would engage your brain?.

KEY QUESTION:

To what extent are you experiencing your favorite aspects of yourself?

Go back through your list on the previous page. Put a checkmark beside those things that are front and center in your life.

Circle anything that is less evident in your current life. *For example, if you love your spirit of adventure but notice you're not being very adventuresome these days, circle that item.*

Next, focus on each circled item, one at a time. Ask yourself: given my current life situation, how can I express this more? *For example, if you used to be a world traveller but now are a working mom, what opportunities might there be for family adventures?* Make some notes here:

The purpose of these activities is to remind you of your favorite facets of yourself, to acknowledge those aspects you are expressing regularly, and to flag those features that may require more attention.

This is where the opportunities for real change happen: when you can (a) identify parts of yourself you enjoy that are not being adequately expressed, and then (b) find ways to express them more in your current life.

The more you give adequate attention to whatever aspects you enjoy most about yourself, the more you will like yourself.

FIELDWORK ACTIVITY:

Pick one favorite aspect of yourself that is not currently receiving enough attention. How could you express it more this week? *For example, if one of your favorite things about yourself is your creativity, then declare this to be the Week of Creativity: Indulge in your favorite artistic endeavors. Make new things. Dress more distinctively. Devise more exotic meals. Brainstorm innovative solutions to any problems you encounter. Make a point of getting to a gallery or a craft store or a musical performance.*

BONUS ACTIVITY:

Going forward, devote each subsequent week to another favorite aspect of yourself. Look for ways to embrace, indulge, and demonstrate this part of yourself.

PHASE THREE: LIKE YOURSELF

Key Question: Do I Appreciate What I've Done?

Part of liking yourself involves recognizing and appreciating your achievements. Before concluding this chapter, remind yourself of what you've accomplished thus far in your life. This might include:

- things you've done of which you are proud
- goals you've reached
- challenges you've overcome
- problems you've solved
- things you've created
- successful relationships (personal and professional)
- prizes, awards, badges, certificates, diplomas, degrees, credentials, etc.
- key life milestones (e.g., acquiring jobs, homes)

ACTIVITY:

List at least ten things you've accomplished or achieved.

➢
➢
➢
➢
➢
➢
➢
➢
➢
➢

SELF-WORTH ESSENTIALS

BONUS ACTIVITY:

List ten more things you've accomplished or achieved.

-
-
-
-
-
-
-
-
-
-

Ж

Chapter 6

Phase Four: Respect Yourself

The more you like yourself, the easier it is to respect yourself. The more you respect yourself, the better you will treat yourself. This is the focus of this chapter.

Ж

Key Question: How Do You Treat Yourself?

How are you treating yourself these days? Consider different areas of your life. Be candid and specific.

KEY QUESTION: HOW DO YOU TREAT YOURSELF?

1. To what extent are you taking good care of your body? What are you doing to bolster your physical health?

2. What are you doing that is unhealthy?

---

3. To what extent are you taking good care of your mind? To what extent are you learning and developing?

4. What are you doing to bolster your psychological well-being and mental health?

5. How do you tend to talk to yourself? What is the tone of the little voice in your head?

6. To what extent are you taking good care of your spiritual needs? To what extent are you participating in whatever spiritual practices you find fulfilling and soothing?

7. How much "you time" do you give yourself each day?

   Each week?

8. Review your answers to the questions 1 - 7. Put a checkmark beside ways in which you are taking good care of yourself. Circle any opportunities for improvement. In what ways could you treat yourself better?

If you already treat yourself well, excellent! Kindly proceed to the next chapter. If, however, you would like to treat yourself better, keep reading.

You are worth treating well.

If you have any doubts about this fact, consider this: You are a human being doing the best you can with the skills, information, and resources you have available. This has been true for every moment of your life. Consider all you've accomplished and achieved in your life. (If in doubt, review your answers on pages 31 and 32.)

You deserve to be treated well. You deserve to treat yourself well. Right now, you can decide to do so. Here's how:

Six Ways to Treat Yourself Well

1. Put yourself first

Do you put yourself first? If you're like most people, you don't. You run around juggling too many projects, responsibilities, and random life demands. You ignore or downplay your own needs. You put other people's needs ahead of your own (e.g., your boss, your family, your co-workers, your friends).

It may seem counter-intuitive but the better way to serve others is to put yourself first. There's a reason why airlines instruct passengers to "put on your own oxygen mask first before assisting others with theirs." You can't help anyone else if you've passed out from lack of air. In the same way, you can't tend to all the people, projects, and responsibilities on your plate until you first attend to your own needs.

DEEP DIVE ACTIVITY: PUT YOURSELF FIRST

What if I told you to stop what you're doing RIGHT NOW and put yourself first. What would be your reaction? Relief (*Gosh, you mean I can?*), incredulity (*You must be joking! I can't possibly!*), anger (*How dare you even suggest it?*), frustration (*I'd really like to but there's no way I can*), fear (*If I change, things might fall apart!*), guilt (*That would be selfish*) — or something else? Write down your gut response.

Why do you think you responded that way? Whose voice(s) do you hear in your head? What unhelpful beliefs are preventing you from putting yourself first? It might sound like any of the following: "If I don't work myself to the bone and struggle with ever fiber of my being, I won't earn my success." "Nice people put others first." "A good parent/spouse/colleague puts themself last." "I don't have time to read/exercise/meditate." "There aren't enough hours in the day to attend to all aspects of my life properly."

Take a few moments and write down your key unhelpful beliefs in the chart below.

As you do so, generate evidence to the contrary. For example: "Well, come to think of it, there is no law that says one must struggle to succeed. I tend to do much better when I'm enjoying what I do, actually. And when I look around at my friends who are doing well — and my role models — they're not stressed out, pushing. They're not being martyrs. In fact I think my martyrdom has hurt some of my relationships."

My Unhelpful Beliefs	Evidence to the Contrary

Phase Four: Respect Yourself

Now consider the costs of NOT putting yourself first. How does it affect you and the people around you? (If you get stuck, consider your answer on page 35. It may provide a clue.)

Key Question:

What are the costs of NOT putting yourself first?

Have you experienced a lopsided relationship (personal or professional) — or muted your ideas or skills unnecessarily — or played the "Doormat" role? I'm sure your intentions were noble. Perhaps you are a "People Pleaser." It's one thing to be kind, respectful, and helpful…it's quite another when you allow others to take advantage of you…or get swept away by their needs, losing sight of your own. This kind of victimhood isn't an effective way to serve others.

If you really want to help others, you need to put yourself first. When you do so, you are in a better position to attend to the needs of everyone else. So really, you owe it to the other people in your life to put yourself first.

How can you put yourself first? By making a conscious decision to honor your own needs.

KEY QUESTIONS:

1. What's important to you?

2. What makes you happy?

3. What is gratifying to you? What makes you feel fulfilled?

4. Review your answers to questions 1 - 3. Put a check mark beside each item that is getting sufficient attention in your current life. Circle anything that isn't.

5. What adjustments need to be made, going forward?

6. How can you remind yourself of your top priorities, going forward?

2. Listen to your body

Your body always knows what you need. It detects when you're hungry or thirsty or sleepy or in danger. Being attentive to your biological needs is a fundamental part of putting yourself first. If you're feeling stressed or achy or fatigued, pause for a moment. Ask your body what it needs: It might be a walk or a nap or an apple…or a week on a beach.

As well, your body can cut through the confusion when too much is going on. Our brains can hijack our actions and attention in a million directions, built on a thousand random rationales. But a "gut feeling" is infallible. If you listen to your gut, it will reveal which is the best idea; which path is crazy making and which is a delight; which person is dangerous or draining and who is a kindred spirit. If you find yourself over-thinking things, try listening to your gut instinct.

FIELDWORK ACTIVITY: WHAT DOES YOUR BODY NEED?

Clear ten uninterrupted minutes. Scan each part of your body, bit by bit. As you focus on each individual segment, seek to detect what it needs in this moment: A change in temperature? A change in activity? A change in position? A certain food or beverage? Sleep? Something else?

Whatever it is, make a point of accommodating your body's needs to the extent possible.

FIELDWORK ACTIVITY:

Going forward, repeat this activity once a day.

---

3. Feed your brain

Your brain yearns to learn and grow and develop. When you avoid learning, your brain cells atrophy and you have less to contribute to your personal and professional life.

What would you like to learn? Consider topics you'd like to know more about as well as skills or techniques you'd like to hone or acquire. Include professional as well as personal interests.

SELF-WORTH ESSENTIALS

KEY QUESTION:

What would you like to learn? Make a list.

FIELDWORK ACTIVITY:

Pick one thing on your list. Spend at least an hour this week learning.

FIELDWORK ACTIVITY:

Go to www.youtube.com. Type in any question. Learn something new.

KEY QUESTION:

Going forward, how can you make learning a regular part of your life?

4. Monitor your mind

How do you talk to yourself? What kind of messages tend to replay in your mind? What's your tone like? Are you harsh or supportive of your efforts?

Do you call yourself names or berate yourself needlessly? If so, you need to address your Inner Critic. It says things like, "This is no good" or "I'm an idiot" or "Who do you think you're kidding?" Your Inner Critic does not respect you. You must teach it to respect you by putting it in its place when it surfaces.

It may sound like someone from your past — or it might not. I call my own inner voice Picky McStrict. My coaching clients use names like "Sir Harps-a-lot", "Ursula", "Poopyhead", "Nick the Dick", "Lady Gwendolyn", "El Stupido", and "Mr. Dibbs My Grade Two Teacher."

Often, our Inner Critics raise or highlight false beliefs. The more these negative statements get repeated, the more we tend to believe them. It's important to recognize them and dispute them whenever we hear them.

For example, if your Inner Critic is saying "I'm too old to make it as a saxophone player", step one is to recognize that this is not objectively true i.e. this is a false belief.

Step two is to contest it. Generate as much evidence to the contrary as you can. (E.g., "I know several successful sax players who recorded their first CD when they were much older than me. I'm a better player now than I was ten years ago. It's only too late if I give up now.")

Step three is to replace it with a more helpful belief. For example: "I am becoming a successful saxophone player."

Now, write down everything you can think of to support this preferred belief. (E.g., "I'm a good musician; I book regular gigs; I've received praise from professionals I admire; I know I'm better than that group I heard at Jazz Fest — if they got their CD made, so can I.") Make a compelling case for any belief that will support you in your endeavor.

Let's begin by examining your Inner Critic. What does it say? How does it say it? Does it sound like anyone you know? Of what is it afraid?

Once you get a sense of your Inner Critic, give it an appropriate name so you can call it out — and laugh at it — when you recognize it. For example: "I realize you're nervous about the client presentation, Sir Harps-a-Lot. But you're making me unnecessarily anxious. I'll do a much better job if you'd kindly leave me to it."

DEEP DIVE ACTIVITY: YOUR INNER CRITIC

1. What kinds of things does your Inner Critic tend to say?

2. What tone does your Inner Critic use?

3. Who does your Inner Critic sound like?

4. Of what is your Inner Critic afraid?

5. Name your Inner Critic so you can call it out — and laugh at it — when you hear it.

    Henceforth, I shall call my Inner Critic_____

Phase Four: Respect Yourself

List the False Beliefs your Inner Critic tends to raise in the column below:	What evidence is there to the contrary? What's the real truth here? Write as many refutations as possible.	What alternative beliefs would you prefer?	What evidence supports your preferred beliefs? Be compelling!

5. Nourish your spirit

Some people enjoy participating in organized religious services or rituals. Others seek solace in spiritual practices such as prayer or meditation or expressing daily gratitude. Some people are soothed by spending time in nature. For what does your spirit yearn?

KEY QUESTION: WHAT DOES YOUR SPIRIT NEED?

Reflect on your spiritual needs and the extent to which you are meeting them.

What adjustments need to happen, going forward?

---

6. Give yourself "you time"

As human beings, we need social relationships and activities. We also need private time. The more demands on us, the greater the need for some uninterrupted time to focus on ourselves at least a little every day.

Yes, you are very busy. And yet there are ways to give yourself time. As busy as you are, you are no doubt spending excessive time on things that really, when you stop and think about it, are not that important to you. You may be surfing the web or noodling around Pinterest or dabbling in social media more than you need to be.

You may be doing things you don't actually have to do yourself. As you go through your day, ask yourself: Do I really need to do this? Does it need to be done? If yes, who else could do it? Can I delegate it? Can I pay someone else to do it?

KEY QUESTIONS: "YOU TIME"

1. Given your current life, what "you time" can you arrange for yourself?

2. What are you currently spending time on that you could delegate to others or pay someone else to do?

3. What are you currently spending excessive time on? What could you be doing more efficiently or spending less time on?

4. What habits could you curtail to give yourself time for more important things? *Consider things like watching television, web surfing, and time spent on social media.*

5. If you really had to, how could you find yourself more "you time"?

Putting It All Together

It can be overwhelming to consider all the ways in which you could be treating yourself better so let's pause here to put things in perspective. The point of this chapter is to devise doable, practical ways in which you can treat yourself well, given your current life situation.

What could you reasonably do to treat yourself better? It might be a matter of eating a salad a day or giving yourself fifteen minutes after work to unwind or finding a way to spend time in nature once a week. Whatever you can do, you are signaling to yourself that you deserve to be treated well. You are proving to yourself that you merit respect.

DEEP DIVE ACTIVITY: TREAT YOURSELF WELL

Consider your unique situation and preferences. Answer the following questions:

1. Given your current life, what's one thing you could do to take better care of your body?

2. Given your current life, what's one thing you could do to take better care of your mind?

3. Given your current life, what's one thing you could do to take better care of your spirit?

FIELDWORK ACTIVITY:

This week, practice implementing these actions.

Going forward, check in with yourself once a week. Are you doing these things to take better care of yourself? If yes, pat yourself on the back. If no, what adjustments need to be made?

Chapter 7

Phase Five: Be Confident in Yourself

Once you like and respect yourself, you are in a position to be confident in yourself. This means knowing who you are and what you can do. This requires

- valuing your core competencies
- doing things for your own approval, rather than for the approval of others
- overcoming fundamental fears and self-doubts

Ж

Valuing your Core Competencies

If you've been working through the activities in this book, this section should be a pleasant review and confirmation of what you already know about yourself.

KEY QUESTION: WHAT ARE YOUR CORE COMPETENCIES?

1. What are you good at? What are your strengths?

2. What comes as naturally to you as breathing?

3. What key skills and knowledge have you developed?

4. For what abilities do you receive the most compliments?

5. Review your answers to questions 1 – 4. Of these, pick three that you know are absolutely true for you. *For example, Beth knows without a shadow of a doubt that she is smart, creative, and organized. Colin knows that he is calm, adventuresome, and generous.*

   ➢

   ➢

   ➢

The three items you chose in answer to question #5 are your Core Competencies. These are your three key strengths. Any of them give you an advantage. When used in combination, they create your unique point of power.

When presented with new situations, opportunities, or challenges, you are not beginning from zero. You bring to the party the best parts of yourself. You can apply your Core Competencies to any new situation, or experience.

PHASE FIVE: BE CONFIDENT IN YOURSELF

DEEP DIVE ACTIVITY: RELYING ON YOUR CORE COMPETENCIES

1. Think of an incidence in which you faced a personal crisis. How did your core competencies help you?

2. Think of a time you entered an unknown situation. How did your Core Competencies help you?

3. How do your Core Competencies help you professionally?

4. How do your Core Competencies help you socially?

FIELDWORK ACTIVITY: RELYING ON YOUR CORE COMPETENCIES

Going forward, whenever you encounter new or challenging circumstances, pause. Remind yourself of your three Core Competencies. See how you can apply them to the situation at hand.

Doing Things for Your Own Approval

When we are young, it's natural that we seek approval from our families and other people around us. Hey, we're trying to get the hang of all aspects of life! We couldn't do that without feedback.

As we grow and develop self-confidence, however, we can cease to fret and worry about what others might think.

When we are confident in ourselves, we can do things to please ourselves, rather than others.

We can defend our ideas effectively when others see things differently.

We can take pride in something we know is good — regardless of what the critics or anyone else says about it.

The challenge is that some of us become dependent on the approval of others. In extreme cases, nothing we do matters unless it is validated by someone else.

KEY QUESTION:

To what extent do you need the approval of others?

On a scale of one to ten, in which "1" means "not at all" and "10" means "a lot", answer the following questions:

To what extent do you do things to please yourself? _____

To what extent do you do things to please others? _____

To what extent are you comfortable defending your ideas when others see things differently? _____

To what extent are you comfortable receiving criticism? _____

To what extent do you find it easy to pursue your own path in the face of opposition? _____

To what extent to you need your efforts to be validated by others? _____

You know best if this is an issue for you. If you are relatively immune to the opinions of others, please proceed to the next chapter.

If, however, you crave others' approval and are at the mercy of their opinions, you have an opportunity to improve your self-confidence. To the extent you do, the easier it will be to foster your self-worth.

Are you a People Pleaser? We mentioned this in Chapter Six. If the intervening activities have not shifted things — if you are still attending to the needs of others at a cost to yourself, then you have an opportunity to pause and address this pattern. I highly recommend *The Disease to Please* by Harriet Braiker. Take time to work through the ideas and activities in her book, then come back here to resume this workbook.

Are you focused on others' opinions because you don't respect your own? Perhaps you harbor fundamental fears and self-doubts. If so, the next section is for you.

Overcoming Fundamental Fears and Self-Doubts

What concerns you? What makes you worry? What causes you stress or anxiety? Deep down, what is your biggest fear?

Your clever mind wants to protect you so it tends to shield you from your deepest, darkest fears with smaller worries, anxieties, and concerns. Just as an archeologist needs to dig through some layers of debris to reveal what's hidden beneath, it's helpful to sift through surface concerns as a way of illuminating what's going on underneath.

Let's begin by sorting through the different ways fear may be manifesting in you.

On the next page is a Deep Dive Activity to explore your key fears and self-doubts. Clear some uninterrupted time. The idea is to complete the sentences as fast as possible — without editing or judging. Begin with the first sentence fragment and complete it numerous times, quickly. When your responses peter out, move onto the next sentence fragment and repeat the process. Carry on down the page.

DEEP DIVE ACTIVITY: IDENTIFYING KEY FEARS AND SELF-DOUBTS

As fast as you can, complete the following sentence fragments. Begin with the first one and complete it several times before moving onto the next.

I'm nervous that…

I worry about…

I'm afraid that…

I'm anxious about…

I'm concerned that…

I'm fearful . . .

I'm frightened…

I'm terrified…

Reread what you wrote on page 52. What do you notice? What stands out for you?

As soon as you recognize a fear that is true for you, address it.

First consider how it is affecting you and those around you. What is it costing you? What stress have you experienced because of this fear — and what stress have you imposed on others? What opportunities have you missed?

What benefits is it giving you? How has this fear helped you in your life? What have you avoided?

Once you understand the role of a particular fear in your life, you can assess it and refute it. Is it actually true? How valid is it? What evidence is there to the contrary?

What follows is a process to address your fear. If you'd like to work through more than one, feel free to make photocopies of page 54. Make enough copies that you can work through each fear separately. I recommend that you work through only one fear on a given day. Pace yourself gently.

DEEP DIVE ACTIVITY: ADDRESS YOUR FEAR

Today I will focus on this fear:

1. How does this fear affect my life today? How does it manifest?

2. How does this fear affect the people close to me?

3. What protection has this fear given me? How else has this fear served me well in my life? What benefits am I presently getting from this fear?

4. What is this fear costing me? What is the impact on my self-worth?

5. What would be the benefits of overcoming this fear?

6. Is this fear even mine? Is this really my fear or is it the concern of someone else close to me — or society as a whole?

7. Is this fear valid? Is it really true? What evidence is there to the contrary? What is the real truth here? What is the objective reality? *Write out as many refutations as you can.*

8. What would I rather believe? *Be specific and detailed.*

PHASE FIVE: BE CONFIDENT IN YOURSELF

Addressing Fundamental Fears

It is quite likely that deeper, more Fundamental Fears underlie the concerns you identified in the previous section. To the extent we dig deeper, we can better understand what's going on — and overcome it.

Fundamental Fears are worst-case scenarios: They are the sources of pain we hide deep inside. They include things like:

- I'm afraid I don't deserve success, love, or security
- I'm afraid I'm worthless
- I'm afraid I'm a failure
- I'm afraid I'm unlovable
- I'm afraid I'll end up destitute

DEEP DIVE ACTIVITY: IDENTIFY YOUR FUNDAMENTAL FEAR

Re-read the list of Fundamental Fears above. As you do, make note of what is especially true for you. Which gives you the biggest reaction? Which stings the most?

What is your Fundamental Fear? Write it down in your own words.

Now here's the good news: **Your fundamental fears are not true.** To the extent you can dispute them, you can dispel them.

We'll do so by expanding the process we used in the previous section: By understanding the impact of this fundamental fear on you and the people around you, by challenging it, and by refuting it with the truth.

DEEP DIVE ACTIVITY: ADDRESS YOUR FUNDAMENTAL FEAR

1. How does this Fundamental Fear affect my life today? How does it manifest?

2. How does this fear affect the people close to me?

3. What protection has this fear given me? How else has this fear served me well in my life? What benefits am I presently getting from this fear?

4. What is this fear costing me? What is the impact on my self-worth?

5. What would be the benefits of overcoming this fear?

6. Is this fear even mine? Is this really my fear or is it the concern of someone else close to me or society as a whole?

7. Is this fear valid? Is it really true? What evidence is there to the contrary? What is the real truth here? What is the objective reality? Write out as many refutations as you can.

8. What would I rather believe?

Reread your answers above. Circle the most helpful statements you've made.

Use them to create a "Truth List" enumerating reasons your Fundamental Fear is false. As you think of other helpful statements, add them to your list. Keep it somewhere handy yet private — on an index card in your wallet; on a list in your phone, computer, or table; on sticky notes — whatever works for you.

FIELDWORK ACTIVITY: READ YOUR TRUTH LIST

For the next thirty days, make a point of re-reading these statements at least once a day. Even better if you do so aloud.

Counter Your Fears

Susan Jeffers, Ph.D. has made a career out of helping people overcome fears by taking action. In her terrific books she explains that EVERYONE is afraid, so it's no biggie that you are. Your fear will grow until you take action. So...*Feel the Fear and Do It Anyway*. (That's the title of her first book. I encourage you to check it out.)

Dr. Jeffers' recommended mantra to overcome fear is to remind yourself that "whatever happens, I'll handle it." She advocates countering fear-inducing "what if's" with "I'll handle it."

For example:

What if I get sick? I'll handle it!

What if I lose my job? I'll handle it!

KEY QUESTION:

What are the "what if's" that are most distressing for you? For each, think about it. Should this thing happen, it might be unpleasant, it might be challenging . . . but you *would* get through it. You've dealt with everything you've experienced so far in your life . . . and you *will* handle whatever else comes up.

On the lines below, write some "what if's" that concern you. As you write each item, immediately say out loud, "I'll handle it."

What if_____? Answer: I'll handle it!

What if_____? Answer: I'll handle it!

What if_____? Answer: I'll handle it!

What if_____? Answer: I'll handle it!

What if_____? Answer: I'll handle it!

FIELDWORK ACTIVITY:

Going forward, when you sense fear, make a point of telling yourself, whatever it is you're experiencing, you'll handle it.

PHASE FIVE: BE CONFIDENT IN YOURSELF

Invalidate your Fundamental Fears

Think about this: Deep down, everyone is afraid. EVERYONE bears some Fundamental Fears. YOU now have the advantage of recognizing what's going on. Very few people ever do.

Once you identify your own Fundamental Fears and see how they are affecting you — especially how they are affecting your self-worth — you can take steps to render them impotent.

You can choose to act despite your fears, rather than because of them.

You can choose to prevent your fears from defining you or controlling you.

You can choose to reject your fears.

You can choose to laugh at your fears — or to giggle when you notice them.

Going forward, how would you prefer to respond to your Fundamental Fears, when they arise?

FIELDWORK ACTIVITY: INVALIDATING YOUR FUNDAMENTAL FEARS

How would you prefer to respond to your Fundamental Fears when they arise? Write out some specifics. *(E.g., find the humor in the situation, remind myself that this sensation does not define me, etc.)*

Make yourself a card with statements to invalidate your Fundamental Fears. Choose from among the following basic truths, then add others unique to your situation:

I am safe.
I am loved.
I am worthy.
I deserve success, love, and happiness.
Whatever happens, I'll handle it.

Going forward, when you experience fear, read your card. (Read it aloud, if possible.)

Ж

Important Note:

Addressing Fundamental Fears can be an iterative process. From time to time, your fears may revisit you — and new ones may burble up. Whenever they do, work through the activities in this section. Each time you do, you'll discover new insights.

Ж

Chapter 8

Phase Six: Enjoy Yourself

When you know yourself so well that you respect yourself and have confidence in yourself, you can truly enjoy yourself. You can delight in yourself. You can celebrate what's important to you. You can give yourself permission to play.

Ж

Enjoy Yourself

The easiest way to enjoy yourself is to do more of what you love — and less of what you don't.

Somehow random things in life can hijack our time and energy. If we're not attentive, we can find ourselves inadvertently short-changing the things we love.

What do you love? This might include:

- specific activities
- spending time in certain circumstances or locations
- using particular skills or talents
- listening to your favorite sounds
- eating your favorite foods
- connecting with certain people

KEY QUESTION: WHAT DO YOU LOVE?

1. Make a list of things you love.

2. Review your answers to question 1. Circle whatever is important to you.

3. What is currently a part of your regular activities that you do not enjoy? Make a list. Also review your answers to the "You Time" questions on page 45.

4. Given your current life situation, how could you do more of what you love, and less of what you don't? What adjustments can you make, going forward?

PHASE SIX: ENJOY YOURSELF

Another way to enjoy yourself is to simply delight in being you – to indulge in what you love best about yourself.

FIELDWORK ACTIVITY: ENJOY BEING YOU

1. If your mission this week was to enjoy being you, what would you do? Make a list.

2. Devise ways to do as many things on your list as possible this week.

3. Do them.

FIELDWORK ACTIVITY:

Make a point of enjoying yourself every day this week.

Celebrate What's Important to You

Do you take time to commemorate the people, places, and events that are truly important to you...or do you tend to let things slide without giving them much consideration? Do you celebrate your accomplishments or do you gloss over them and run straight to the next thing on your "to do" list?

An important part of developing your self-worth is to value what's important to you and to celebrate it accordingly. Besides, it's a wonderful way to Enjoy Yourself.

Consider any of the following:

Personal Days - *to do whatever you wish or whatever you need*

A true personal day is a gift you give yourself. When you take a Personal Day, the idea is to ask yourself, "What do I really, truly need *today*?" Maybe you need to nap. Or to spend the day in your PJs, watching schlock TV. Are you yearning to spend a day in nature? Are you feeling so behind on something that it would be a relief to spend a day getting caught up?

Play Days - *devoted to having fun*

What's fun for you? It might be a day trip. Eighteen holes. A jaunt to the beach. Hours exploring art galleries.

Priority Days - *devoted to attending to your current personal priority*

What is your overriding priority these days? It might be to relax more – or to spend more time with your family – or to upgrade your skills. Whatever's most important to you, why not devote a day to that priority? For example, if "Family" is your current top priority, why not plan a Family Fun Day? If "Learning" is your main concern, you could schedule classes or workshops or reading days.

Celebration Days - *to honor important events*

These might be traditional . . . birthdays or anniversaries or calendar holidays. Or they might be celebrations of your own devising. What would *you* like to honor? What qualities or accomplishments or anniversaries or traditions would you like to commemorate?

For example, I like to celebrate the anniversary of the day I defended my doctoral dissertation. It felt like a big accomplishment to earn my Ph.D. before the age of thirty. It was made more meaningful because family and friends drove for five to eight hours to be there. Their smiling faces were sprinkled throughout the audience when I presented my data to the department. We had a terrific party that night, too — tasty eats and fun festivities. In the years since, I've made it a point to recognize and celebrate this personal anniversary.

FIELDWORK ACTIVITY:

1. Right now, pick up your calendar and put a big star on (at least) four random days during the year. When those days roll around, make a point of enjoying a Personal Day, a Play Day, a Priority Day, or a Celebration Day.

2. While your planner is out, highlight important events, birthdays, or anniversaries. This year, make a point of making them true celebrations.

ACTIVITY : CELEBRATE YOUR ACCOMPLISHMENTS

1. In Chapter Five you were invited to make a list of your achievements and accomplishments. Review your answers on pages 31 and 32.

2. Make notes beside each item to indicate to what extent you celebrated it.

3. What pattern do you see? Do you tend to celebrate your accomplishments or do you tend to gloss over them and head straight onto the next thing?

4. How would you prefer to operate, going forward?

5. Pick something you can aim to celebrate in the near future. What upcoming project milestone or completion could you acknowledge? How would you like to do so?

6. Make a point of doing so.

Note: This section is adapted from my book *Making the Most of Your Milestone Birthday: 52 Ways to Have the Best Year Ever*. It contains many other ideas to foster celebration in your life.

Give Yourself Permission to Play

In the previous section, you were encouraged to schedule Play Days. What was your reaction? Did you leap at the idea or did you scoff? If you have plenty of playtime in your life, kindly skip ahead to Chapter Nine. If you don't, please continue reading.

A surprising number of people don't play very much at all. They are juggling so many projects, ideas, and life demands that they don't allow themselves much, if any, playtime.

Play is important. It's fun. It gives us energy. It sparks ideas. It enhances creativity. It gives us joy. Every young mammal plays. It's part of being alive. Of interacting with others. Of learning new behaviors.

What happens among people, however, is that many of us are told, at some point to "grow up." To "get serious." To "stop playing around." Most of us bow to societal pressure. Some of us impose restrictions on ourselves — limiting our playtime or doling it out it a miserly fashion, perhaps as a reward for certain achievements. At some point, many of us just don't play anymore.

How about you? First, what do you consider "play." What's fun for you? What are your favorite ways to play? Janet loves to dance. Hank adores computer games. James likes flying kites. Kim enjoys surfing. I get a kick out of playing hide and seek with my dogs.

FIELDWORK ACTIVITY: MAKE A PERSONALIZED PLAY LIST

1. Take a moment to create your personalized "Play List": What are your favorite ways to play? What's fun for you?

> 2. Go through your list on page 66. Beside each item, write down the last time you did it.
>
> 3. Review your list. What do you notice? Any surprises? What patterns do you see?

Would you benefit from more play in your life?

If you start to balk — if you're reaction is along the line of, "I can't possibly" or "I have too much to do" or "I'll play when I'm retired" — consider the benefits of regular play.

1. Play gives you energy.

If you feel sluggish or stressed out or otherwise "icky", odds are you need more play in your life. Once you give yourself the gift of regular playtime, you will have more energy to tackle your personal and professional responsibilities.

2. Play gives you ideas.

If you are stuck or slogging through a project, some playtime can create a shift in perspective to get you moving or to spark a fresh approach.

3. Play enhances your creativity.

The more you play, the more innovative you can be.

4. Play improves your relationships.

Play makes you happy. When you are happier, you are more pleasant to be with. Your personal and professional interactions are more positive.

5. Play is an antidote for procrastination.

If you are avoiding doing something, it might be because you've made the task into something onerous or "Very Important" or otherwise terrifying. To the extent you can shift your attitude to "Okay let me just play around with this a bit," you can nudge yourself into moving forward. Play lets you take action from a more positive, less fearful place.

6. Play is an antidote for perfectionism.

If you tend to be hard on yourself — if you tend to set high expectations of yourself and others — you know the pain of perfectionism. You sit down expecting to make "something excellent." This sets up a dynamic so that whatever you are trying to create is being judged at its very genesis. This is crazy-making. It's impossible to simultaneously generate new thoughts — and keep them coming — if you are jumping all over them, judging them as soon as they emerge.

A different approach is to compartmentalize. First, allow yourself some playtime to generate — without judgment. Go ahead and slap down some paint, jot down that first draft. Just get it out there. Play around with whatever tickles your fancy. Have fun with it. Then, when the generation phase concludes, revisit your project to assess and hone as needed.

Ж

Whether or not you believe in the value and benefits of play, why not give it a try? Add some playtime to your week this week. See what happens.

FIELDWORK ACTIVITY:

This week, make a point of playing every day. If this is a challenge for you, commit to play at least five minutes every day.

BONUS ACTIVITY:

If there is something on your "Play List" you haven't done for a while, make a point of doing it this week.

Now let's say, it's a week from today and, somehow you didn't play. At all. For whatever reason, you didn't give yourself even five minutes of playtime.

What interfered? What stopped you?

Take a moment and answer honestly.

Maybe life intervened. Perhaps you had way too much going on. I'd like to challenge you on that. Surely there were ways to inject some play into the tasks at hand. Certainly you could give yourself five minutes to play a bit of *Pokemon Go* or a round of backgammon or to try doing a cartwheel in the backyard.

Phase Six: Enjoy Yourself

Maybe it's guilt. Do you need permission to play? Do you feel that you haven't yet "earned" your playtime? Allow me to help: Because you've read this far, you have absolutely earned at least five minutes of play every day for the next week (and, actually, for the rest of your life).

Let's try the activity again.

FIELDWORK ACTIVITY:

This week, make a point of playing every day. If this is a challenge for you, commit to play at least five minutes every day.

BONUS ACTIVITY:

Play at least five minutes a day, every day, for the next year. See what happens.

Ж

Chapter 9

Phase Seven: Love Yourself

Think about what it feels like to love someone else — a friend or a family member or a romantic partner. Contemplate the emotional component — the joy and comfort you feel when you're near them, for example. Consider how you think of them (i.e. fondly and frequently). Reflect on what you do for them. These acts of love might include checking in on them often, spending time with them, giving them gifts, saving them from things they don't like, and facilitating what they do like.

Loving yourself is much the same. When you love yourself

- you are happy to be you

- you are happy to keep yourself company

- you think well of yourself

- you check in frequently with yourself

- you treat yourself thoughtfully

- you give yourself gifts

- you forgive yourself

Let's begin this essential phase by focusing on the last item on this list.

Ж

Forgive Yourself

Love mandates forgiveness. No one is perfect. When you love someone, you love them, flaws and all. You forgive them their failings as you expect them to forgive yours.

Self-worth requires that you extend yourself the same courtesy. Are you good at forgiving yourself? If so, please skip ahead to the next section.

If not —if you are hard on yourself or tend to punish yourself for the "mistakes" you've made — please read on: Forgiving yourself is a key component of valuing yourself and loving yourself. If you insist on carrying negative experiences from your past, you are pointlessly denying yourself happiness in the present. You are limiting your capacity to love and value yourself unconditionally.

You deserve to be treated kindly and compassionately — especially by yourself. As human beings, we all make mistakes. Whatever it is, forgive yourself. You deserve the same courtesy you would give someone else. Imagine the relief of truly forgiving yourself. Picture yourself laying those unnecessary burdens down…and moving forward with your life. Rather than berating yourself for things you can't change, wouldn't you prefer to be spending that energy on something more pleasant, healthy, or helpful?

DEEP DIVE ACTIVITY: FORGIVE YOURSELF

Clear some uninterrupted time for private reflection.

1. Make a list: For what do you need to forgive yourself?

2. Pick one item from your list on page 72. Answer the following questions:

- What does it cost you to carry this burden? How does it affect different areas of your life? Your relationships? Your attitude?

- What does it cost others around you?

- What benefits would there be to forgiving yourself? How would you feel? How would it change how you are living your life?

- What's been stopping you from forgiving yourself? Why are you denying yourself this relief?

- What can you do to forgive yourself?

3. Take a moment. Acknowledge that you are a fallible human, that you make mistakes and that you deserve forgiveness for them. That you do the best you can at any given moment, given your skills, knowledge, and understanding at that time. View yourself with compassion and kindness. Picture yourself as a small child. Forgive yourself.

4. Make photocopies of the activity on page 74. On another day, pick a different item from the list on page 72. Clear some uninterrupted time and fill out one of the photocopied pages.

5. Repeat #4 until you have addressed every item on list on page 72.

DEEP DIVE ACTIVITY: FORGIVE YOURSELF

Photocopy this page to use as needed. Clear some uninterrupted time for private reflection.

1. What is something for which you'd like to forgive yourself?

2. What does it cost you to carry this burden? How does it affect different areas of your life? Your relationships? Your attitude?

3. What does it cost others around you?

4. What benefits would there be to forgiving yourself? How would you feel? How would it change how you are living your life?

5. What's been stopping you from forgiving yourself? Why are you denying yourself this relief?

6. What can you do to forgive yourself?

7. Take a moment. Acknowledge that you are a fallible human, that you make mistakes and that you deserve forgiveness for them. That you do the best you can at any given moment, given your skills, knowledge, and understanding at that time. View yourself with compassion and kindness. Picture yourself as a small child. Forgive yourself.

> **FIELDWORK ACTIVITY:**
>
> Going forward, whenever something arises that requires it, forgive yourself.

Be Your Own Best Friend

Our true friends support us and encourage us. They reassure us that we're okay, our ideas are sound, our projects are worthwhile, and our talents are considerable. They check in on us. They help us through our challenges. They celebrate our triumphs.

We can learn a lot from our friends.

> **KEY QUESTION:** YOUR BEST FRIEND
>
> Name one good friend: _____
>
> With that person in mind, answer the following:
>
> 1. How do they treat you, on a daily basis?
>
> 2. How do they speak to you?
>
> 3. How have they helped you during difficult times?
>
> 4. What things have they done or said that demonstrates their friendship and affection for you?

SELF-WORTH ESSENTIALS

5. What support do they give you?

6. How do they express appreciation for you?

7. What gifts do they give you?

KEY QUESTIONS: BE YOUR OWN BEST FRIEND

1. Going forward, how can you be your own best friend?

2. What are you already doing that works well?

3. What can you do differently?

4. What opportunities for improvement are there?

DEEP DIVE ACTIVITY: LETTER OF ENCOURAGEMENT

Clear some uninterrupted time. Write yourself a letter of encouragement as if you were your best friend.

FIELDWORK ACTIVITY: BUY YOURSELF A GIFT

1. This week, make a point of buying yourself a present. Choose your gift with care. What's something you'd really enjoy and appreciate? What would be a treat?

2. Wrap it (or have it wrapped) attractively.

3. Hide it somewhere in your home where you will stumble upon it in the near future.

FIELDWORK ACTIVITY: TAKE YOURSELF ON A DATE

Plan an enjoyable outing. Pick something that would be fun and special for you. Dress up for yourself.

Actually go on your date.

BONUS ACTIVITY:

Repeat this activity at least once a month.

Moving Forward

I hope you've found this book helpful in understanding yourself better, treating yourself well, and valuing yourself more. Your stories, feedback, and suggestions for improvement on this book are most welcome. Please contact me here: **bit.ly/contactliisakyle**

Many of my readers find they'd like more support and personalized help in improving their self-worth. I offer **three month coaching packages** tailored to accomplish your specific goals, no matter where you are in the world. Working with me, using a dynamic combination of live one-on-one phone or Skype sessions, personalized fieldwork activities, and email support, in just 90 days you can:

- ✓ figure out what you really want — and what you really don't
- ✓ achieve your goals faster, easier, and with less stress
- ✓ identify and overcome whatever has been holding you back or interfering with your success
- ✓ overcome obstacles you encounter more effectively, more efficiently, and more easily
- ✓ do more of what you love and less of what you don't
- ✓ manage your time more effectively and efficiently
- ✓ gain a deeper understanding of your core strengths and learn how to make the most of them
- ✓ acquire a better understanding of different areas of your life and how to make real improvements in them
- ✓ achieve an improved work/life balance
- ✓ improve your personal and professional relationships
- ✓ enjoy your life more

I've helped people make real, significant changes in their life — and I'd love to do the same for you. Tell me how I can help. Simply fill out this short online form to let me know what you'd like to get out of coaching, your preferred contact information, and any relevant info you'd care to share: **bit.ly/contactliisakyle**

Note: Your information is 100% confidential and filling out the form doesn't commit you to anything.

Wishing you all the best,

Liisa Kyle, Ph.D.

About the Author

Liisa Kyle, Ph.D. is the go-to coach for smart, creative people who want to overcome challenges, get organized, get things done, and get more out of life. She's coached individuals, facilitated groups, and delivered inventive workshops on four continents. (www.LiisaKyle.com, www.CoachingForCreativePeople.com)

She's also an internationally published writer/editor/ photographer. She's authored books about

- happiness
- creativity
- getting things done
- goal-setting and planning
- self-worth
- overcoming procrastination
- overcoming perfectionism
- getting over regrets, disappointments and past mistakes
- how to make the most of a milestone birthday, and
- how to make real, directed, personal change.

She earned her Ph.D. in Psychology from the University of Michigan.

Liisa Kyle co-founded The DaVinci Dilemma™ — an online community devoted to helping smart, creative people juggling too many talents, too many projects, and too many ideas. Check out her free self-help articles at www.DavinciDilemma.com.

She lives in the Pacific Northwest with her multi-talented spouse, a snuggly Yellow Lab, and a Labradoodle who looks like a *Dr. Seuss* character.

To arrange personal one-on-one coaching, corporate consultation, workshops, or public speaking appearances: bit.ly/contactliisakyle

Free Weekly E-Mail Self-Coaching Prompts: bit.ly/weeklyprompts

Coaching Special Offers: bit.ly/LKspecialoffer

Books by Liisa Kyle, Ph.D.

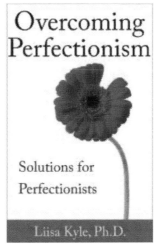

 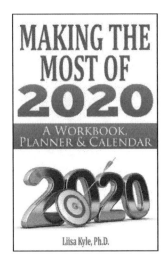 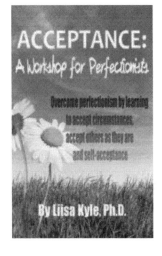

Made in the USA
San Bernardino, CA
19 November 2019